FAMILY W9-BIR-241
P. O. Box 1442
02-1442

THE TASTE OF OUR TIME

Collection planned and directed by

ALBERT SKIRA

HISTORICAL AND CRITICAL STUDY
BY
ROBERT L. DELEVOY

Translated by Stuart Gilbert

Family of Faith Library

BRUEGEL

Title page:
The Procession to Calvary, detail: Boy crossing a Stream, 1564.
Kunsthistorisches Museum, Vienna.

★

Distributed in the United States by
THE WORLD PUBLISHING COMPANY
2231 West 110th Street, Cleveland 2, Ohio

★

© by Editions d'Art Albert Skira, 1959.
Library of Congress Catalog Card Number: 59-12319.

The spelling of proper names was erratic in the 16th century. Bruegel, at first, hesitated between two forms: "Brueghel" and "Bruegel." Only in 1559 did he definitively adopt the second. We never find his name spelt "Breughel" or "Breugel." The spelling followed in this volume corresponds to the one most commonly employed by the artist.

*

So as to make our reproductions of Bruegel's vast, encyclopedic compositions easier to decipher, we have thought it best, departing from our general rule, to present on double pages those containing an exceptionally large number of figures.

TWO MEN IN BACK VIEW. PEN DRAWING.
CABINET DES ESTAMPES, BIBLIOTHÈQUE ROYALE DE BELGIQUE, BRUSSELS.

THE LIFE OF BRUEGEL

AN UNCLEAR PROFILE

> What does he mean to me, this man who steps in
> between humanity and myself?... It is not he, it is
> nature, it is humanity working at a given point in time
> and space that is the true author.
>
> ERNEST RENAN.

T HE scenes and incidents that Bruegel has recorded in his
drawings, prints and pictures still supply us with the best
means to an understanding of the successive phases of his life.
For despite the unflagging efforts of an impressive number of
art historians during the last half century, little or no progress
has been made towards defining the somewhat unclear profile
of the artist given by Carel van Mander, in 1604, in his famous
Schilderboek. The skeleton biography compiled by that eminent
chronicler of early Netherlandish painting lacks some key
pieces of information which all the industry of erudite research-
ers has so far failed to uncover or reconstitute. We have only
conjectures to go on as to the master's birthplace and the date
of his birth, the social background of his early years, how and
when he took to painting, the time he came to Antwerp, the
exact itineraries of his travels, the real reasons for his move to
Brussels and the circumstances of his early death.

True, a precise knowledge of the facts might (as so often
happens in such cases) tend to give undue prominence to
anecdotal elements and submerge essentials in a mass of that
"factual" apparatus whose limitations—narrowness of outlook,
tameness and triviality—are only too familiar to us. Since,
however, individual experience is always bound up with
collective experience, we shall find in the latter a compensation
for the lacunae of the former. Those very lacunae, in any case,
have stimulated research work and critical scrutiny of the

œuvre itself to such effect as to lend color to the view expressed by Rabindranath Tagore: that in such cases all that is most important lies outside the artist's personal vicissitudes, his manner of living and day-to-day events—all, in short, that would normally figure in a full-length biography.

Broadly speaking, then, Bruegel's life story is largely a matter of guesswork, and approximative at best. This did not, however, cramp the prolific imagination of a Flemish writer, Felix Timmermans, author of a *vie romancée* of the artist which has been translated into several languages and of which the least that can be said is that it displays a singular disregard for truth. All the fully authenticated evidence available, so far anyhow, consists of five documents dating to the master's lifetime: an entry in the lists of a painters' guild; two letters written by the Bolognese geographer Scipio Fabius, dated June 16, 1561, and April 14, 1565; a record of Bruegel's marriage in the register of Notre-Dame de la Chapelle at Brussels; a brief mention of him by Guicciardini in 1567. If it could be proved that the name "Meesteren van Pieter Bruegel" which figures in the minutes of a meeting of the Brussels City Council that took place on January 18, 1569, refers to him, we should have a sixth piece of documentary evidence, informing us that at this time Bruegel was exempted from having Spanish soldiers quartered on him and was given a sum of money.

The first of these documents is a sadly laconic but invaluable entry in the registers of the Guild of St Luke at Antwerp where the name *Peeter Brueghels, schilder* appears along with those of thirty-six painters, engravers and craftsmen admitted to membership in 1551. This is conclusive proof that a certain "Peeter Brueghels, painter" existed and was at Antwerp during the reign of the Emperor Charles V. Though this official, colorless, objective entry, figuring as it does between the names of an engraver, Ghisi, and a painter, Martin van Cleve, may seem at first sight as unrevealing as a regimental number, something may be gleaned from it. For it contains what is generally accepted as a clue to the painter's place of origin, since the "s" at the end of the name can be taken as an adjectival termination, meaning that the "Peeter" in question hailed from a place named Brueghel.

On this view, our "Peeter," lacking a family name—as was common at the time, especially among the peasantry—decided to adopt as his surname the name of his birthplace. But exactly where this was is still a moot point. For there are no less than three ancient villages with the name Brueghel (or Brögel). One is in the former Duchy of Brabant some sixty miles from Antwerp and a little over five miles north of Eindhoven; it now belongs to the parish of Son (in present-day Holland) and boasts of a modern monument to the memory of the painter. The two other (adjoining) villages, Kleine-Brögel and Groote-Brögel, situated some thirty-six miles south of the Brueghel in Holland, are a little over three miles away from the small town of Brée. Formerly they lay within the principality of Liège, but they are now included in the Limburg province of Belgium.

All three are situated in the region, common to Belgium and Holland, known as the Campine. This is a wide expanse of moors and heather, sand and meadows, polled willows and fir plantations, that becomes slightly hilly west of the Dutch village, where there are some small stagnant lakes, dating perhaps to very ancient times. Allowing for the changes this region must have undergone with the passing centuries, I should be inclined to accept the views of Edouard Michel who on the strength of some of Bruegel's landscapes (drawings and paintings) claims to see distinctively "Bruegelian" qualities in the Dutch countryside, were it not that the Brabantine countryside in the neighborhood of Brussels also has, even at the present time, many of the same characteristics. Moreover there is nothing to justify us in assuming that after leaving his (presumed) native place in very early youth, Bruegel ever had occasion to return to it.

In this context we do well to bear in mind the positive assertion made by one of his contemporaries. In his celebrated *Descrittione di tutti i Paesi Bassi*, published in 1567, Ludovico Guicciardini definitely states that Pieter Bruegel hailed from Breda. This statement was partially endorsed thirty-seven years later by Van Mander, who tells us that Bruegel "was born not far from Breda in a village named Breughel, a name he took for himself and handed on to his descendants."

Actually there does not exist, and has never existed, a village in the neighborhood of Breda bearing the painter's name; the three villages of that name are some forty-four and thirty miles distant from Breda. This led Van Bastelaer to put forward the theory, which has much to commend it, that the "Breda" to which Guicciardini and Van Mander referred was in reality the small town of Brée, near which are the two villages named Brögel. Brée was, in fact, once called Brede and, in Latin, Brida and Breda (see Van Bastelaer and Hulin de Loo, *Peter Bruegel l'Ancien*, Brussels 1907, p. 145). As a result of recent investigations by Charles Bossus, it is now established that the name of this town was spelt Breda in 1078, Brida a year later, Briede in 1335, Brede in the 15th century and, in the 16th and 17th centuries, Bréda; it was not till the next century that the name Brea and its present form, Brée, came into currency. Moreover, in 17th-century documents the name "Groote-Brögel" was written "Breughel."

Finally, due weight should be given to the widely current oral tradition that the painter was born in the large, centuries-old farmhouse at the place named "Ooievaarsnest" (Stork's Nest) in the parish of Groote-Brögel, two or three hundred yards distant from the small road connecting Brée with the market town of Peer. This farmhouse was partially destroyed by fire in 1866, but it has been rebuilt according to the original plan above a masonry substructure that may well go back to the 13th century. It would seem that in the 16th century the farm belonged to the de Hornes family, and Charles Bossus has suggested that Count Philippe de Hornes, subsequently one of the Duke of Alva's many victims, may very well have noticed the young peasant's talent and supervised his artistic training. M. Bossus carries his theory, which rests on the slenderest foundations, a stage further and would have us believe that, thirty years later, Bruegel joined with his former patron in the northerners' revolt against their Spanish overlords. He thinks that he has thus "definitively" established the birthplace of Pieter Bruegel the Elder. Unfortunately a local tradition, no less positive and persistent than the Belgian tradition mentioned above, attaches to the Dutch village Brueghel-Son, and according to it the painter was a foundling who was adopted by a family of peasants living on a farm which no longer exists today and which, too, had the name of "Ooievaarsnest." The parish priest, struck by the boy's talent, arranged for his training at Eindhoven where (again according to the legend) he sold some of his first drawings and made for the local church a copy of "The Disciples at Emmaus." In short, the early history of this great artist is, as so often happens in such cases, enveloped in a mist of conflicting legends.

For after this recourse to the sources, we can but admit that the central problem remains unsolved, or anyhow obfuscated by "a cloud of unknowing." True, the probabilities are strongly in favor of the view that Groote-Brögel in the neighborhood of Brée (also known as Breda) was our painter's birthplace. Yet allowance must be made for the fact that the records of the Guild of St Luke usually specify the places of origin of artists who have no patronymic by adding the word "van" and the name of a locality (e.g. Joos van Cleve, Pieter van Aelst,

Jan van Venloo, Jan van Mechelen, *et al.*). And there is nothing to prevent our regarding the vocable "Peeter Brueghels" not as an adjectival form but as a genitive: meaning "Peeter son of Brueghel," not "Peeter hailing from Brueghel." Color is lent to this conjecture by the fact that several persons of almost the same name are known to have existed in the 16th century; there was a Canon Michael Breughel at Antwerp, a doctor at Brussels styled in a Latin text "Magister Bruegelius," and a certain "Guillaume van Breughel" was a prominent figure at the Court of Brabant. Also, at Amsterdam, a poet, Gerrit Hendriksz. van Breughel, is recorded as being a member of a Chamber of Rhetoric in the early 17th century. No connection between these persons and the painter's family has so far been traced. Finally—to make confusion worse confounded—we have to bear in mind the fact that persons having a family name sometimes added a topographic surname, such as Bruegel (see Van Bastelaer, *op. cit.*, p. 145). Thus, all efforts notwithstanding, we are left in the dark as to the local and social background of one of the greatest artists of all time. Perhaps indeed there is more wisdom in the skeptical smile with which the Limburg farmer at Ooievaarsnest greets the enthusiastic pilgrim than in the hasty conclusions of some of our art historians.

The lack of documentary evidence makes itself felt no less acutely when attempts are made to ascertain the date of Bruegel's birth. The only reliable clue we have is the entry in the records of the Antwerp painters' guild. It is generally held that an artist had to put in six years' apprenticeship before he qualified as a "free master." Ever since, in 1890, Henri Hymans advanced the theory that this period of training began when the candidate was fifteen to seventeen years old, art historians have assumed that when Bruegel was admitted as a master in 1551 he must have been about twenty-three, i.e. that he was born around 1528. This chronology may, however, be slightly modified.

For there were very few artists who qualified as masters at such an early age. Rubens was an exception. Pieter Coeck and Joachim Beuckelaer were twenty-five, Jan Metsys and Gonzales Coques twenty-six, Pieter Aertsen was twenty-seven and "Velvet" Brueghel twenty-nine. We should be more inclined to assume exceptional precocity in Bruegel's case, were it not that one of his most brilliant contemporaries and a personal friend of his, Abraham Ortelius, tells us that the "most absolute" (i.e. perfect) painter of his century—a fact that could be gainsaid "only by enviers and ignoramuses"—died in 1569 "in the flower of his age" *(medio aetatis flore)*, meaning what was then regarded as the medial point of a man's active life, his forty-fifth year. This would imply that Bruegel was born about the year 1525 and was twenty-six when he obtained his "master's degree"— an estimate supported by the two or three extant portraits showing him at the height of his powers and representing a man seemingly in his early forties. In the present state of our know-ledge, any more precise estimate would be imprudent, and there is little hope of clearing up the matter. Thus the assertion made by Charles Bossus in an article in the Gazette des Beaux-Arts (February 1953, p. 126) to the effect that he believes he can fix "with absolute certainty" the year of Bruegel's birth as 1522 seems rash, to say the least of it.

Any survey of Bruegel's career up to 1551 can be little more than a series of almost unanswerable queries. What were the social and cultural origins of this painter whom we may fancy we know so well—so popular has he become—but who has in fact guarded his secret so intriguingly? Where and how, one wonders, did he acquire the habit of scanning the world with a gaze so eager and so ruthless? What of the early years of this many-sided genius? Did he go directly to Antwerp from his hometown or did he begin by trying his chance elsewhere? True, we know that the answers to these questions could not have any bearing on the essential values of his work. Yet they would be reassuring after a manner, would satisfy legitimate curiosity and—best of all—might put a stop to idle speculations about the man and his message.

It is in that excellent source book, Van Mander's *Schilderboek* (published in 1604), that we have the first piece of information (somewhat late in date, however) about Bruegel's activities in the years before he qualified as a free master. Van Mander tells us that "he learnt his craft from Pieter Coeck," and this is confirmed by Coeck's biographer, Franciscus Sweertius, who says that Coeck "had a pupil, the painter Pieter Bruegel, to whom he gave his daughter in marriage." This statement is generally accepted and some have sought to corroborate it by pointing to alleged traces of Pieter Coeck's decorative style in Bruegel's work. But these resemblances are dubious at best. Indeed, in a general way, it may be said that when art criticism uses suppositions of this order to bolster up some preconceived hypothesis, it tends to lose its authority and dwindles into mere verbiage. Yet Charles de Tolnay is almost the only writer on the subject who declines to see traces of any such influence in Bruegel's art. All the same, we cannot follow him when he goes on to use this as an argument against the reliability of Van Mander's account of Bruegel's life. On the contrary it helps us to understand the psychology of the youthful artist, both the precocious maturity of his talent and the uncompromising independence of his character. For a young man needed a strong, decided personality of his own if he was to stand up to the ascendancy of a teacher so gifted as Pieter Coeck, a copious (if rather prolix) painter, a man of wide-ranging knowledge, a very fine scholar, translator of the treatises on architecture of Vitruvius and Serlio, himself an architect and a highly esteemed designer of tapestry cartoons. All Coeck's work was imbued with the Italianizing formalism then considered the acme of good taste. At most one may perhaps be justified in seeing the influence of the tapestry designer in the markedly vertical structure of Bruegel's earliest large-scale compositions, *Netherlandish Proverbs*, *Carnival and Lent* and *Children's Games*. Similarly some authorities believe they can account for the topographical precision of his larger landscapes by the fact of his being a close friend of Ortelius, that "learned and admirable mathematician who with much honor to himself and to the satisfaction of all has figured forth the Theater of the entire terrestrial globe." But analogy hunting of this kind, however ingenious, seems of little real service for an understanding of the artist. We probably do better to dispense with such theories, based as they are on vague resemblances, and to view the artist's œuvre in a broader context, capable of showing how far it was conditioned by the spirit of the age he lived in and contemporary problems.

It is greatly to be regretted that Van Mander fails to specify the exact date when Bruegel came to study under Pieter Coeck. The first period of Coeck's brilliant but very brief career was spent in Antwerp. Brother-in-law of the painter Jan van Amstel, he married after the death of his first wife a famous miniature painter, Mayken Verhulst. In 1544 there began a new phase of his life, when he was summoned to Brussels to take over the post of the court painter Bernard van Orley, who had died in 1541. This did not, however, lead him to sever his connection with Antwerp, and when and where he enrolled Bruegel as an apprentice remains an open question. Did he do so at Antwerp, before 1544, or at Brussels? In other words, did Bruegel go to Brussels before settling in Antwerp? In any case—Van Mander is once more our informant—he went to work in the studio of the Antwerp master, Hieronymus Cock, after the untimely death of Pieter Coeck (which took place on December 6, 1550). It is quite possible that Bruegel was a member of the group of two hundred and thirty-five artists who in the previous year, under Coeck's supervision, had made the decorations of the City of Antwerp for the visit of Charles V and his son Philip.

In short, we may well believe that the young painter fell under the spell of the "City of the Seven Gates" in the course of his stay there. Antwerp was now a flourishing international and cosmopolitan center, a focal point of world trade and, as Guicciardini described it, "the common fatherland of all the Christian nations." While Bruges, stronghold of a defunctive conservatism, was losing its pre-eminence, Antwerp, greatly daring, had cast off the shackles of a parochial economy and given free play to the new forces of capital and private enterprise. German, Italian, Spanish and Portuguese businessmen, immigrants from all the dominions of the Emperor Charles V, had settled in the city where they now could benefit by the most complete commercial freedom and the most fully developed economic system of the age.

"Indeed," Guicciardini goes on to say, "it is wonderful to see such a concourse of men of so many different humors and qualities; and still more wonderful to come on such a variety of languages so different from each other, so that without traveling abroad you can observe in a single town (and, if you so desire, imitate exactly) the ways of living and customs of diverse distant nations." So typically middle-class was the social climate at Antwerp that few of the nobility deigned to reside there. Nonetheless the citizens lived luxuriously, "perhaps more so than good sense would justify. At every hour of the day there are banquets, weddings, dances and sundry entertainments. In every street you can hear the sound of musical instruments, songs and merry-making. At every turn, in fact, you find tokens of the wealth, the pomp and power, and the splendor of this fine, most eminent City." Moreover, the Antwerp merchants showed "a well-nigh unbelievable activity in buying and selling, and warehousing commodities of all descriptions."

Alongside a busy traffic in oriental spices, grain from the North, French wines, German metals and English cloth, there developed an equally busy and prosperous picture market, stocked with works of art of all sorts and sizes hailing from every part of Europe. To begin with, the scene of its activities was the "Kerkplaats," near the cathedral; when the space available there proved insufficient, the market was transferred in 1540 to an upper floor of the New Stock Exchange. Guicciardini says that works were often purchased there "sight unseen," before delivery, and whole cargoes of pictures were assembled on the premises for shipment to Spain. Of the painters, engravers, sculptors and others supplying the Antwerp market with their wares some three hundred had qualified as "masters," and as such been granted official licences for the sale of their productions. Antwerp was also famed for its printing works; not only were more than half the books published in the Low Countries printed there, but it had become, like Paris and Frankfort, the center of a thriving trade in prints. Those published by Georg Hoefnagel, Willem and Hans Liefrinck, Philipp Galle, Hendrick Goltzius, Gerhard de Jode, the Wierixes and others were exported en masse to Italy, Spain and France and in even greater numbers to Spanish America. Meanwhile the same dealers—hard-headed businessmen as well as patriots —were importing quantities of engravings of Italian and German provenance. This new development had an influence on the evolution of the Renaissance in the North equaling, to say the least, that of the printed book.

Among the pioneers of the movement the most enterprising was undoubtedly Hieronymus Cock, a painter and a highly expert copper-plate engraver. No sooner had he won admission to the Guild of St Luke (in 1546) than he went to Italy, staying from 1546 to 1548 in Rome. A lengthy mention of Cock in the *Lives* testifies to Vasari's high regard for him. What he saw in the Roman print shops and the establishments of the great publishers of prints—Antonio Lafreri, Tomaso Barlacchi, Antonio Salamanca, Claudio Ducceti and Giacomo Rossi—made him realize the enormous possibilities of this new industry. As a result, on his return to Antwerp, he decided to launch an enterprise of the same type on his own account. Accordingly he founded a publishing house near the New Stock Exchange, at the corner of La Courte rue Neuve and the Rempart Sainte-Catherine, giving it the auspicious name of "In de vier Winden" (At the Sign of the Four Winds). And before long his establishment became the rallying point of the best artists of the day, headquarters of a brilliant school of engraving, and a favorite meeting place of the intelligentsia. Henceforth the House of the Four Winds was to share the Europe-wide prestige of Plantin's famous "Golden Compass." When we remember that Cock's father had taken the lead in making Hieronymus Bosch's art known in Antwerp; that one of Hieronymus Cock's earliest ventures was to have engravings made of the works of that brilliantly original genius and thus bringing them to the notice of a wider public; and, finally, that this great publisher's program evidences a desire to strike a judicious balance between the creations of local artists in the popular tradition and those of the Italian masters—when we bear these facts in mind, there can be little doubt about the part played by this milieu in the shaping of the Bruegelian *ars poetica*. Though no great stress need be laid on the fact that Bruegel is certain to have met the Mantuan engraver Giorgio Ghisi at the "Four Winds," it is highly probable that this encounter strengthened his desire to make the usual "pilgrimage to Italy" —which we may well imagine was proposed to him in the first instance by his employer. In that case, it may also be surmised that Hieronymus Cock asked his young assistant to carry out some artistic or commercial research work while in Italy.

However this may be, it is certain that in 1553 Bruegel was in Rome. This is proved by two etchings inscribed *Petrus Bruegel fecit Romae Aº 1553*, and here again we have a confirmation of one of Van Mander's statements. These are two landscapes of the panoramic type in the tradition of Patinir and his followers. To them may be added a much finer work which, though undated, is signed *Bruegel* and inscribed *a Roma*. This, a pen drawing of the *Ripa Grande* (in Rome), now in the Duke of Devonshire's Collection, Chatsworth, is a work whose vibrant calligraphy premises a sensibility of a quite exceptional order.

It is from Rome, again, that we glean some information regarding Bruegel's painterly activities at this time. In the catalogue, dated June 22, 1668, of the Collection of J. B. Borrekens at Antwerp is an entry: "fragment of a picture painted by Bruegel at Rome" (see J. Denucé, *Les Galeries d'art à Anvers aux XVIe et XVIIe siècles*. Catalogue, p. 256). This entry is of much interest, historically speaking, since it informs us of the young artist's earliest ventures in the field of painting. He must have already given proof of quite unusual talent and technical proficiency for him to have attracted the attention of Giulio Clovio, the famous miniaturist whom Vasari described as *un piccolo e nuovo Michelagnolo*. From the inventory of Clovio's estate we learn not only that Bruegel collaborated with him on occasion but also that he presented his Italian friend with at least three of his works, listed as *Una torre di Babilonia di avolio di mano di Mro Pietro Brugole; Un quadro di un albero a guazzo di Mro Pietro Brugole; Un quadro di Leon di Francia a guazzo di mano di Mro Pietro Brugole*: i.e. a *Tower of Babel* on ivory, a picture of a tree in watercolors and a view of Lyons, also in watercolors. Clovio's will (December 27, 1577) also mentions these works, all of which unhappily are lost.

It was not due to chance that Bruegel took to miniature painting when in Rome. He must have had many opportunities of learning this technique, since Pieter Coeck's wife, Mayken Verhulst, was a highly proficient miniaturist. So here we have an indirect confirmation of the fact of Bruegel's apprenticeship to the great Flemish decorative artist.

Bruegel, it would seem, turned out a vast quantity of work during his stay in Italy, mostly in the form of drawings and engravings. The hasty sketches in which he recorded his day-to-day discoveries of the Italian scene provided him with a fund of first impressions, dashed off in the rapture of the moment, on which he was to draw all his life long. There can be no doubt that what most quickened his youthful sensibility and delighted his eye was far less the hallowed vestiges of the past than the natural beauties of the southern landscape. His thirst for new visual sensations and his indefatigable curiosity led him to explore the furthest south of Italy. Gustav Glück recently discovered a view of Fondi (Private Collection, U.S.A.), a small town midway between Rome and Naples. That Bruegel visited Naples is proved by that famous picture, the *Harbor of Naples* (Galleria Doria, Rome). Though it is unsigned, its resemblance to his drawing of the *Roadstead of Antwerp* (c. 1550, Private Collection, London) is unmistakable.

Next we find our painter in Calabria, where he made the drawing *View of Reggio* (Boymans Museum, Rotterdam, formerly in the Koenigs Collection), a delightful work where the fine, nervous, pointillist pen-strokes are supplemented by touches of lightly applied color, added later and said to be the work of Claude Lorrain. Here we have undoubtedly a preliminary study for that remarkable composition, the *Sea Battle in the Straits of Messina* of which, in 1561, Hieronymus Cock had an engraving made by the highly expert etcher Frans Huys. The composition is so skillfully built up touch by touch and to it the artist has evidently devoted so much loving care that we are fully justified in believing that in its original form it was a large-scale painting, all trace of which has been lost. Linking up with the striking series of *Ships of the Sea* (also engraved by Frans Huys after drawings made in Sicily), this print, an exceptionally large one, has an obvious documentary interest: that of recording a dramatic naval engagement in the Franco-Turkish struggle for supremacy in the Mediterranean. Also, it marked the beginning of a genre of painting (hitherto confined to miniatures) that was brought to fruition and standardized in the following century by the Dutch painters Bakhuysen and Willem van de Velde. (An intermediate stage in the development of the genre can be found in an album of sketches—MS 22089 in the Bibliothèque Royale, Brussels—several of which quite clearly stem from Bruegelian sources.)

Bruegel seems to have followed an oddly circuitous route on his journey to Rome. The mention of a view of Lyons in the inventory of Clovio's estate is held to be proof that he visited that city on his way. Thence he presumably followed the Rhone valley, stopping at Geneva, before tackling the arduous crossing of the Alps. Resemblances have been traced between certain localities in the Rhone valley and the landscapes of *Hunters in the Snow* and the *Magpie on the Gallows*. Also, the landscape of the *Harvesters* (Metropolitan Museum, New York) might well be a view of Geneva seen from the village of Archamp; the profile of the mountain range in the far distance, the indentations of the lake and the general layout of the plain are remarkably like the view one has today from the foot of the Salève (a mountain near Geneva). Finally, in the famous "Large Landscape Series" engraved, it seems, by Cock in 1555, Louis Lebeer claims to have identified Mont Salève, some of the Savoie mountains, a view of Chillon, the countryside between Aigle and Bex, Mont Catogne and the Dent du Midi.

A drawing of the *Ticino Valley* (Dresden), the mention of a lost picture, "Mount St. Godard *(sic)* by Bruegel the Elder," in the Rubens Collection (Denucé, *op. cit.*, p. 64) and a drawing inscribed *Walterrspurg* (at Bowdoin College, Brunswick, Maine) which Otto Benesch has recently identified as a view of Waltensburg in the Canton of Grisons, Switzerland, give some further clues to the wanderings of this singularly erratic traveler. Lastly, mention may be made of a sketch (in Berlin) which has been thought to represent the Martinswand, a mountain near Innsbruck, but its authenticity is too doubtful to warrant the assumption that Bruegel also visited the Austrian Tirol.

Relatively little is known about the personal contacts made by the artist during his Italian sojourn. Besides striking up a friendship with Clovio, he made the acquaintance of the geographer Scipio Fabius in Rome or Bologna. Evidently the two men took to each other, since some years later in a letter dated June 16, 1561, to Ortelius, Fabius asked for news of his "very dear" friend "Petrus Bruochl." And again, on April 14, 1565, Fabius requested Ortelius to convey his friendly greetings to Bruegel. Reference is also made in these letters to the Antwerp painter Martin de Vos; this has led to a surmise (dubious at best) that the two men joined forces for a part of the journey.

Traveling was an exceedingly slow business in those days, set to the tempo of a day's ride on horseback, and Bruegel's return journey was delayed not only by the difficult country he had to cross but by the movements of armies on the march and sometimes engaged in conflict. At long last "Maestro Pietro Brugole" safely found his way to Antwerp, where we next hear of him in the employ of Hieronymus Cock, at the end of 1553. He collated his travel notes, readied for engraving his "Large Landscape Series" and signed in this same year the first dated painting that has come down to us, the *Landscape with Christ appearing to the Apostles* (Private Collection).

It would seem that for the next four or five years his painterly aspirations were seriously hindered by his activities as a designer for engraving. Under his contract with Cock he was restricted to subjects appealing to contemporary taste, works that could be reproduced in large numbers and catered for the widest possible public. His task was concisely to interpret and to present in visual form and the most telling manner the popular conceptions of the day, in particular the "diabolic" iconography of the great Hieronymus Bosch. But these obligations, due to commercial exigencies and the taste and fashion of the age, were a blessing in disguise since they made constant demands on his imagination and encouraged him to test out his creative powers to the full. No less stimulating must have been his daily contacts at the "Four Winds" with artists of all tendencies, men of letters, intellectuals, dealers and collectors: contacts which go far to explain that "universal" quality which was to be a striking feature of his culture.

As for his political and religious opinions, these can doubtless be gauged by his intimate relations with two distinguished men of the day, Hans Franckert and Christophe Plantin. Connoisseur and merchant, poet and patron of the arts, and a member of the Chamber of Rhetoric named "The Violet," Franckert was an active member of the "Four Winds" circle. A native of Nuremberg, he had migrated to Antwerp owing to his sympathies with the Reformation movement. He was one of Bruegel's first buyers and the frequency and regularity of his commissions must have had a beneficial effect on the artist's productivity. The two men were firm friends. Van Mander tells us that "they often went out into the country to see the peasants at their fairs and weddings. Dressed up as peasants, they brought gifts like the other guests, claiming relationship with the bride or groom." But they could not have got on so well together had they not had many traits in common besides this taste for rustic junketings, and we may assume that they had similar ideas on the problems of the day.

Bruegel's intimacy with Plantin is well-known. Like Hans Franckert, Plantin made no secret of his sympathies with the Reform movement, dangerous as these were. In 1563, having been denounced as belonging to a clandestine sect, he had to flee from Antwerp; this, as it so happens, was also the year when Bruegel left that city and married at Brussels. It has been suggested that he, like his friend, had become involved in some "heretical" movement, and used the wedding as a pretext for moving to a safe distance from potential persecution. Since the circle he frequented seems to have been limited to men of the "Libertine" persuasion, we may draw conclusions as to his own views on such matters and in any case, as we shall see, there are clear indications in his later work that he regarded himself as a "committed" artist. But allowance should also be made for the fact that the financial situation at Antwerp was deteriorating, and this, too, may have prompted him to welcome proposals made by members of the wealthy upper middle class of the "Prinselijke Stad," which was now the political heart of the Low Countries and stepping into the place of Flanders as the arbiter of public opinion. Moreover, as Van Mander tells us, he was courting Mayken, the daughter of his first teacher, Pieter Coeck, at the time and his future mother-in-law was in business at Brussels as an art dealer. According to Van Mander her consent to the marriage was conditional on Bruegel's coming to live in the capital of Brabant "so as to give up and put away all thoughts of his former girl (at Antwerp)." Needless to say, this sentimental reason for his move to Brussels does not necessarily mean that there were not other motives as well, both of a practical order and due to his distaste for the social climate of Antwerp.

The marriage was solemnized in the summer of 1563, in Notre-Dame de la Chapelle, parish church of an ancient working-class district largely inhabited by weavers. This is vouched for by one of the few scraps of documentary evidence dating to the painter's lifetime, the entry

Peeter Brugel

-solmt

Maryken Cocks

in the marriage register of the church in question.

It is generally believed that he lived in the house which now is No. 132 in the Rue Haute, at the corner of the Rue de la Porte Rouge. In the 17th century it formed part of the inheritance of his great-grandson, David Teniers III. It was here that the great painter spent the last six years of his life, years of glory but also of horrified dismay when he saw scaffolds and gallows springing up on every hand, and the air was loud with the rattle of the Spanish musketry.

Two sons were born to him in that darkest period of the history of the Low Countries: Pieter known as "Hell" Brueghel in 1564 (?) and Jan known as "Velvet" Brueghel in 1568. Their father died with tragic suddenness on September 4, 1569, when he was working on a set of pictures that the Brussels City Council had just commissioned to commemorate the completion of the Brussels-Antwerp canal. He was buried near his studio, in the church of Notre-Dame de la Chapelle where his marriage had been celebrated six years before.

That there was every indication of the recently deceased painter's spectacular rise to fame, was the gist of the reply sent by Provost Morillon to a letter from that highly cultured statesman and great art lover Cardinal de Granvella on December 9, 1572. "I sent Christian the painter to buy the xxv paintings on canvas in Antwerp . . . but you must count on having to pay heavily in order to recover the pieces by Breugel." (The archiepiscopal palace at Malines had recently been sacked, in the troubles of 1572.) "Since his death his works are more sought after than ever and they now fetch 50, 100 or 200 crowns."

THE PROCESSION TO CALVARY, DETAIL: A THISTLE, 1564.
KUNSTHISTORISCHES MUSEUM, VIENNA.

THE MEASURE OF ALL THINGS

NATURA NATURANS

> I hold that by *natura naturans* we should mean that which exists in itself and is conceived in itself, in other words such attributes of substance as express an eternal, infinite essence.
>
> SPINOZA.

THE history of Western civilization is far from being all of a piece. Rather, it consists of a series of well-marked phases, a variety of cultural patterns within which the concepts of time and space have undergone far-reaching modifications. Stemming from a complex of interrelations in which science and economics, art and technique, society and the individual, thought and the imagination, reciprocally act upon each other, these modifications reflect, express and illustrate successive changes in the relations between man and society, between man and nature, between man and the universe. These relations are fundamental to the human situation, and determinants of men's outlook on the world in any given period. Thus they involve not only certain habits of thought and ways of seeing but also (as a result of these) certain trends of the creative process. And, finally, they provide fixed criteria that condition, shape and orient the "period" sensibility.

Here begins the work of art: a direct emanation from sensory experience to begin with, but also the expression of an attitude towards the world, "an image of our relationship with nature." Thus the work of art is at once one and multiple, and its unity is apprehended only at the intersection of a great diversity of viewpoints. We need also to extricate it from the rubble of archeology, from the anatomy of styles and the side-issues of erudite analysis. Above all, we need to attune as best we can our modern sensibility to the sensibility which fecundated the work of art at the time of its conception. If this were truly feasible, what a wonderful new world would open up before our eyes! But unfortunately our data are inadequate to furnish a method of approach so stimulating and rewarding. We can only hope that future historians will accumulate the materials needed for a "history of sensibility" through the ages. Then and then only will our understanding of works of art acquire a new dimension and we shall be able to avoid the too widespread tendency to assimilate the vision of the past to ours.

All is in everything; nothing is isolable from the whole. And since implicit in any given fragment, however small, of a completed work is the vibrant life infusing the composition as a whole, the magic power of a detail can never play us false. Take for example this *Thistle*, seen in isolation from the vast, elaborately constructed picture to which it belongs (the *Procession to Calvary*, Vienna, 1564); how well this minor detail summarizes and symbolizes the conception permeating the entire work! Broadly painted, with an amazing sense of tactile values, it reveals in a small compass the mystery of all plant life. It brings before us, in its stark visual actuality, the essential nature of this thick-leaved, spiky plant, flaunting one would say its malevolence to man. But in so speaking we are falling into a common error, and keeping to a critical tradition that should, by now, be obsolete. For it is not the thistle as such that fascinates us, but the element of the human implicit in it, that is to say its revelation of a visual experience and its testimony to a certain state of mind. Seen thus, it is not a mere plant but an upcrop from the deeper strata of consciousness, a transparent symbol summing up the world-view of the epoch.

In that period of unbridled curiosity the vogue for herbals and maps had opened up new fields of interest. And similarly the vogue for automatons pointed the way to the coming of the machine age. Meanwhile, however, time flowed lethargically on

—the "man in a hurry" was as yet unborn. Between its far-flung seacoasts Europe was crossed on horseback or in carriages at an average rate of thirty miles a day. Clocks were just coming into general use, breaking up the flow of organic time—chiefly with a view to fixing the hours of fairs and markets—and introducing an abstract reckoning soon to adjust men's daily lives to a new rhythm. But, as yet, it was the rhythm of nature that prevailed; even within city walls it was the crowing of cocks that announced the hour of waking. After nightfall all was darkness, all was silence, except when the townsfolk were indulging in a festival or music-loving merchants organized a concert. Many discoveries were made, but technics did not advance *pari passu*; water, wind, draught animals were, as they had been since time immemorial, the only sources of applied power. In short "natural conditions" still set the tempo of human activities.

Devoid of any logical structure and always ready to endorse the supernatural, the thought of the day made but desultory appeals to Reason. Mathematics was now in the ascendant, pointing the way towards a quantitative mentality. After being applied to the measurement of time and yoked to the service of commerce, it now applied to indeterminate space a yardstick that was henceforth to supersede the approximations of the artist's eye. Subjected to its disciplines, that eye at last could marshal appearances in a precisely calculated order and impose on them a rigid hierarchy. Mathematical perspective at once provided the artist with a countercheck on his imagination and, in furthering a cosmic sense of space, inaugurated a new relationship with the outside world giving rise to a whole philosophy of nature. Based on an intensive study of the structure of Nature-in-herself, this method of research culminated in an image corresponding to the world-picture formulated by the natural philosopher, the concept of an infinitely extended, eternal

Br. 4

THE PARABLE OF THE SOWER, 1557. NATIONAL GALLERY OF ART,
WASHINGTON, D.C. (LENT BY THE PUTNAM FOUNDATION).

universe, inseparable from its Maker, a concept which was now
so solidly established that it remained unchallenged until the
end of the 19th century.

It fell to Bruegel to implement this new and ampler measure
of the universe in his art. Between the landscape dated 1553
(Private Collection, cf. de Tolnay, Burlington Magazine, August
1955) and the *Storm at Sea*, his last known work (1568, Vienna),

two intermediate pictures admirably illustrate the transition from the qualitative to the quantitative. These are the *Parable of the Sower* dated 1557 (National Gallery, Washington, formerly Stuyck del Bruyère Collection, Antwerp; replica in the Prado, No. 1964) and a *Temptation of St Anthony* (National Gallery, Washington, formerly Franck Collection, London). They seem to have been painted at about the same time, that is to say soon after Cock's publication of the "Large Landscape" series of prints. The layout of the first-named picture is clearly based on that of the

LANDSCAPE WITH THE TEMPTATION OF ST ANTHONY, C. 1557.
NATIONAL GALLERY OF ART, WASHINGTON, D.C. (SAMUEL H. KRESS COLL.).

LANDSCAPE WITH THE FALL OF ICARUS, C. 1558.
MUSÉES ROYAUX DES BEAUX-ARTS, BRUSSELS.

etching *Milites requiescentes* (Bastelaer, No. 17), and the second, while keeping the rhythm of the print *S. Hieronymus in Deserto* (Bastelaer, No. 7), recalls certain details of an engraving in the same series, *Fuga Deiparae in Aegyptum* (Bastelaer, No. 15).

Foreshadowed by Patinir, the new sense of the organic relationship between man and his environment is given here its fullest possible expression. It underlies the structure of the *Weltlandschaft* ("world landscape"), as Ludwig von Baldass aptly names it, and also indicates a visual approach perfectly adapted to the then widespread desire for knowledge.

In Bruegel's truly superb renderings of the visible world, all conspires, as Valéry might have said, to implement the satisfying effect produced on us by these "semi-natural" landscapes: clarity in the treatment, dynamic contrasts, modulations of the light and a brilliant unity of viewpoint. If we call them "semi-natural," this is only because they associate within the same spatial context, always with perfect coherence, a cottage of the North and a Mediterranean sail, a Flemish belfry and a Calabrian stronghold, a Belgian hillside and an Alpine mountain range, the sodden turf of Flanders and the sun-scarred rocks of Italy, the gentle undulations of a meadow and the "accidental statuary" of a rugged foreshore. Here the most searching individualist gaze is wedded to the "universalism" that was then the order of the day. We find a similar attitude in contemporary scientific literature; the writer often aims at combining in a single work the whole range of human knowledge; whether that work deals with jurisprudence, medicine, economics, or history. For whereas Bruegel, thanks to the sweep of his genius, succeeds in overcoming the disparity of motifs and in completely integrating a host of very different, often conflicting, data, the humanist writers were as yet unable to supply their readers with anything more than a mosaic of ideas and observations without co-ordination or connecting links. "It is not unusual," writes J. Ellul, "to find in 16th-century works on jurisprudence long disquisitions on archeology, theology, psychology or linguistics, not to mention history and literature. We find whole chapters devoted to the practice of magic or maybe Peruvian sociology intercalated in books dealing with high finance or the legislation of the Parliament of Bordeaux."

It is amazing to see in Bruegel's œuvre how the golden thread of a great painter's genius weaves its way throughout the complex pattern of contemporary thought; and how therewith he masters and surpasses it. Yet it is well, also, to recognize

THE TOWER OF BABEL, DETAIL: THE CITY, 1563.
KUNSTHISTORISCHES MUSEUM, VIENNA.

the fact that one of the reasons why Bruegel succeeded in endowing painting with a plenitude and a perfection far to seek in the literature of the day was that he had a greater faculty than any of his contemporaries for evaluating the moral and material components of the age and for expressing himself wholly, unreservedly, through their intermediary.

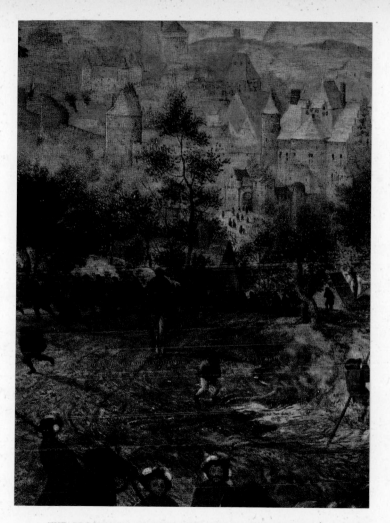

THE PROCESSION TO CALVARY, DETAIL: THE CITY, 1564.
KUNSTHISTORISCHES MUSEUM, VIENNA.

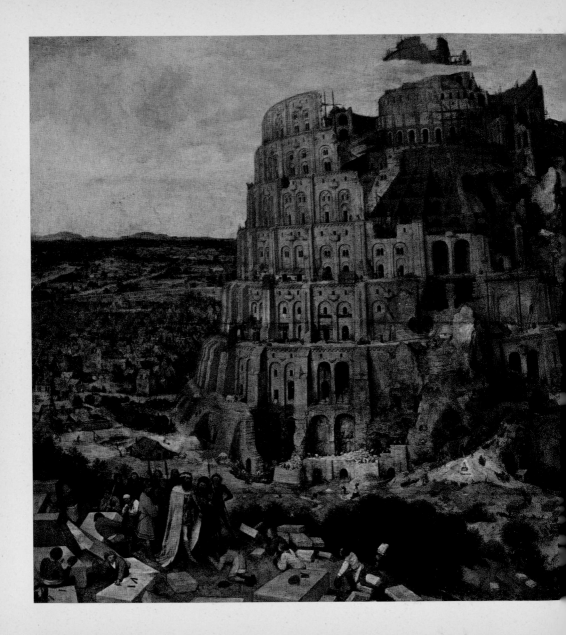

THE TOWER OF BABEL, 1563.
KUNSTHISTORISCHES MUSEUM, VIENNA.

—

Another remarkable feature of these landscapes—to which may be added that ingenious work *The Fall of Icarus* (Brussels, Musées Royaux des Beaux-Arts; another version in the Van Buuren Collection, Brussels) and a *Flight into Egypt* (1563, Count Antoine Seilern Collection, London)—is that they are "composed" with such skill and with such a sense for near-musical effects (single notes, chords and harmonies), and so fluently and effortlessly executed, that we can well believe them to be veritable "slices of nature," directly experienced and apprehended. Here at last an artist has captured in the meshes of the new optics the exact "feel" of ever-changing appearances, sensed the very heart-beats of Nature, and given free rein to a truly impressionist sensibility.

For Bruegel was essentially an open-air man, a lover of the windswept countryside of his native land, as well as a landscape painter born, and we feel this in all his work even when landscape is not the leading theme. True, there was then no thought of painting in the heart of nature; two centuries were to pass before artists had the notion of setting up their easels in open country. But the happy ease of Bruegel's art and the relative truth-to-life of the Bruegelian syntheses are all the more remarkable and precious for this very reason. Nor must it be forgotten that, studio compositions though they are, they are an assimilation of studies done on the spot, scrupulously accurate drawings made *naer't het leven* (from the life) according to the analytic method introduced by Dürer and Leonardo. In them nothing is left to chance. Such is the painter's skill that he submerges the framework—the bare bones—of the composition and the execution of the original drawings under a wealth of masterly brushstrokes, a fluent spate of color, lightly or thickly applied according as it conveys an illusion of space or substantiality, or else (as occasionally happens) is used to mask the emphatic diagonal which often strikes across the three traditional color planes (brown, greenish blue and a bluish grey sometimes flushing into pink, all discreetly modulated). And lastly, so as both to stress the asymmetry of his compositions and to add breadth to his panoramic views, Bruegel took to introducing—this was his personal invention—clumps of trees on the right or left hand side of the picture, which acted as taking-off points for the distribution of the light and the interplay of values throughout the composition.

Ortelius once declared that there was more thought than painting in Bruegel's works—a remark that did less than justice to the artist. True, so eye-filling are these mirrors of the visible, so dazzling is their overall effect, that they seem sufficient to themselves and conceived with but a single aim, that of humanizing nature. Thus it is all the more surprising to discover that underlying all is a motive that today we should style "literary," that all have a biblical or didactic referent and all are charged with a significance discreetly woven into the texture of the composition. The *Parable of the Sower* follows exactly the wording of the passage in St Matthew; the *Fall of Icarus* illustrates a fable in Ovid's *Metamorphoses*; the *Temptation of St Anthony* illustrates an episode of The Golden Legend. All three pictures contain a similar message and go to implement a single train of thought. We see birds pilfering the seed broadcast by the peasant; Icarus failing in his mad attempt to fly; the spirit of evil vainly assailing the hermit. Everywhere action is doomed to failure; and confronted by the inexorable logic of Nature, man learns the limitations of his lot on earth. "*Natura naturans.*" In vain that gigantic *Tower of Babel* (1563, Kunsthistorisches Museum, Vienna; smaller version in the former Van Beuningen Collection, Boymans Museum, Rotterdam) aspires to pierce the sky, never will it scale the zenith, and it remains a monstrous monument to the incorrigible vanity of all human pretensions.

THE BLUE CLOAK (NETHERLANDISH PROVERBS), DETAIL, 1559.
GEMÄLDEGALERIE, BERLIN-DAHLEM.

EVERYDAY LIFE

THE TOPSY-TURVY WORLD

> Every time the world order and the social system
> are called in question this involves an overhaul of the
> résumés of ancient wisdom embodied in the proverbs
> of the past.
>
> CLAUDE ROY.

BRUEGEL'S early drawings and early paintings alike, all dating
to the period between 1553 and 1558, reflected exclusively
the artist's responses to the natural scene: trees and plants,
rivers, plains and mountains, the ocean of the sky, the far-flung
splendor of terrestrial and maritime horizons. By and large they
constituted a full-fledged *ars poetica*, the fruit of daylong medi-
tations, and seemed to point the way towards a boldly experi-
mental art culminating in pure Impressionism.

It was due to Hieronymus Cock that Bruegel's course was
temporarily deflected from this path, and he abandoned poetry
for prose, solitude for collective life, nature for the theater of
the world of men.

As early as 1557 he had begun, at the suggestion of the great
Antwerp publisher, a sequence of seven engravings illustrating
the *Deadly Sins*. Obviously their purpose was to inculcate a
moral lesson. They marked a turning point in his career, away
from a technique all in veiled suggestions to clean-cut linearism,
adapted to engraving. Thus he was called on to superimpose on
his new, still tentative feeling for nature a more "philosophic"
attitude, and also to investigate and exploit the possibilities of
illustrative painting.

Was Bruegel now to yield to literary, medieval, outworn
tendencies, to the didactic pretentiousness of the rhetoricians,
to the encyclopedic pedantry of the humanists? Was he to lapse
into an anecdotal art and surrender to the pressure of tradition?

For if, as his publisher wished, he had now to illustrate the disastrous consequences of men's vices and disclose the motives of their passions, two sources were available and these were bound to tinge his work with archaism and give it a faintly "old-world" air. On the one hand there was the demon-haunted world of Bosch and on the other the copious, familiar repertory of current Netherlandish proverbs. The imagery of the Bois-le-Duc master—his hybrid monsters, obscene creatures, quaint *diableries*—fired Bruegel's imagination. The wit and wisdom of the proverbs appealed to his critical sense, gave scope to his inventiveness and a fillip to his skepticism. Amidst a horde of grotesque, artificial, ambiguous forms, poised in a sort of abstract never-never land, we find a directive idea taking shape, the germ of a new conception of life. The veiled allusions that work their way into the landscapes painted in this same year were not due to chance, but related to the problems that now preoccupied his thoughts. This relationship should be stressed, since it not only shows the adaptability of a highly flexible genius but—what is more important—accounts for the dialectical unity of his later work.

Also commissioned by his publisher was a second series of engravings (begun in 1558), the *Seven Virtues*, designed as a sequel to the *Sins*. But here there is a decisive change of tone. Bruegel has jettisoned the archaisms deriving from Boschian morphology. These pictures of men engaged in the multifarious activities of daily life called for a keenly observant eye, a ruthlessly objective vision. The allegory, central theme round which the composition is built up, is merely a pretext for a vigorous depiction of the mores of the peasantry and townsfolk. In *Faith*, a masterpiece of its kind, Bruegel achieves a style. We see a procession of cowled figures in the nave of a church, all presented in back view and given a single, basic attitude. The setting of *Charity* is a humble village and the central figure is surrounded by peasants of all ages, posed in picturesque, skillfully varied, realistic attitudes; whereas *Prudence* illustrates the homely activities of a housekeeper. By dint of close and constant contacts with reality Bruegel created a *type-figure*, perfectly realized from the very start, and distinctively "Bruegelian," broadbacked, short and sturdy, boldly modeled and fined down to essentials, whose elliptical structure gives only the faintest hints of the geometrical schema underlying it.

From every point of view these drawings are of capital importance. They prove that Bruegel had now formed a habit of thinking in terms of metaphor. He had plunged into the world of fables and proverbs, of the obsessions of the medieval mind and the unrest of the times. These works also led him to the use of close-knit, compact forms, lending themselves to bright, boldly stated local colors. Thus it was not due to chance that he now was led to create his first large-scale paintings based on popular themes. In 1559 he signed and dated two vast compositions: *The World turned Upside Down* (Berlin), better known as *Netherlandish Proverbs*, and *The Fight between Carnival and Lent* (Vienna). In the following year he signed and dated *Children's Games* (Vienna). The three works have approximately the same format and were probably commissioned by his friend the merchant Hans Franckert with a view to decorating the walls of some stately mansion he possessed in Antwerp.

It would seem that in the same two years, 1559-1560, Bruegel painted two equally large panels in the same vein: *Kermess at Hoboken* and the *Joys of Skating*. Both unfortunately are lost, but we get an idea of them from two prints (Bastelaer, Nos. 205, 208). The same fate has befallen the *Witch of Malleghem* and *Madmen's Dance*; the engravings reproducing them (Bastelaer, Nos. 193, 195) show that the painter now was trying to introduce touches of real life into the crabbed accounts of "Human Follies" compiled by the rhetoricians.

THE BLUE CLOAK (NETHERLANDISH PROVERBS),
1559. GEMÄLDEGALERIE, BERLIN-DAHLEM.

The Berlin picture was the first, it seems, of this magnificent sequence. It consists of a pictorial anthology of at least a hundred proverbs, maxims and popular adages reflecting the customs, turns of speech and literature of the Netherlands. A host of figures, including village craftsmen and field laborers with their domestic animals, interpret faithfully each theme. The setting is purely arbitrary, the figures disport themselves on a flat plane, and there are only the faintest hints of perspective recession. The various scenes are treated separately, the only link between them being that of color, a systematic alternation of cool and warm tones. Each of the figures goes his way as if unaware of the others' presence. We see a man winnowing feathers in the wind—an allusion to the saying *want pluymen in den wint*; another seated on ashes between two stools, *tusschen twee stoelen in d'assen sitten*; another trying to knock down a wall by ramming it with his head, *met den kop tegen den muur loopen*; another swimming against the stream; another carrying light in baskets, in broad daylight; and yet another gnawing at a church pillar, while a half-wit makes his confession—to the devil! Lunacy at large, perhaps, but there is a common measure of these follies; all these people are struggling, vainly, to defeat logic, fighting to no avail against the scheme of things. In the center of the composition is a group to which the artist has evidently devoted special attention and which epitomizes all these manifestations of human folly. Here the figure of a young woman in a stylish red dress, falling in Gothic folds, strikes a contrast with the "proletarian" atmosphere of the rest. To prevent his seeing her infidelities she is wrapping round her husband, a lame, tottering oldster, a big cloak with a projecting peak, the "Blauwe Huyck."

Froukens die geern hier en daer den offer ontfangen
Moeten haer mans de blau huycke omhangen.

(The woman who gladly welcomes favors here and there Must hang the Blue Coat round her husband.)

These lines figure under the same group in an engraving by Jan van Doetechum (Joannes a Doetinchum) published at Antwerp in 1577, in which the text of each proverb accompanies the scene illustrating it. Thus it has been of help in deciphering Bruegel's "picture puzzle." It also has an overall caption:

> *De Blauwe Huycke is dith meest ghenaemt*
> *Maer des Werelts Idel sprocken hem beter betaemt.*
>
> (The Blue Cloak is this picture's usual name, but better would be "the Follies of the Topsy-turvy World.")

Recently Louis Lebeer has discovered in the Berlin Kupferstichkabinett a fragment of an etching bearing Frans Hogenberg's monogram and exactly contemporaneous with Bruegel's work. It has the same synoptic layout, with illustrations of twenty-one proverbs, each with its "legend," grouped around the woman "covering her husband with his flowing cloak." Moreover the title of the etching (part of which is lost) was, in its complete form, identical with that of the Van Doetechum print. Finally, the fact that an engraving made at Antwerp in the 18th century and inspired by the same theme is titled (in French) "A True Portrayal of the Follies of the World turned Upside Down" throws additional light on the purport of Bruegel's enormous picture. The "Blue Cloak," psychological, structural and chromatic center of the composition, is an emblem of the folly of a world gone crazy. A folly that the painter neither censures nor commends. He contemplates the antics of his figures with a sardonic smile and tolerant disdain.

In the *Blue Cloak*—it is to be hoped that this more correct title of the so-called *Netherlandish Proverbs* will be adopted—Bruegel, who was grappling for the first time with the problems of a large-scale work, could not entirely cope with its thematic complexity. Not only do the forms still lack concision and often seem a trifle clumsy, but the piecemeal composition and profusion of details tell against a true organic unity.

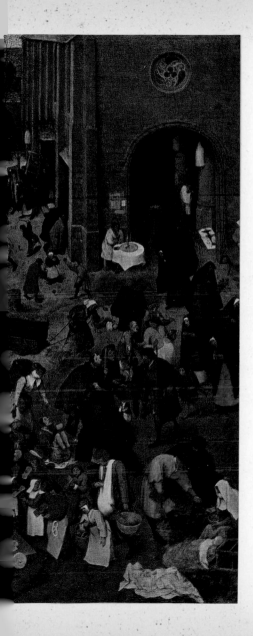

THE FIGHT
BETWEEN CARNIVAL AND LENT, 1559.
KUNSTHISTORISCHES MUSEUM, VIENNA.

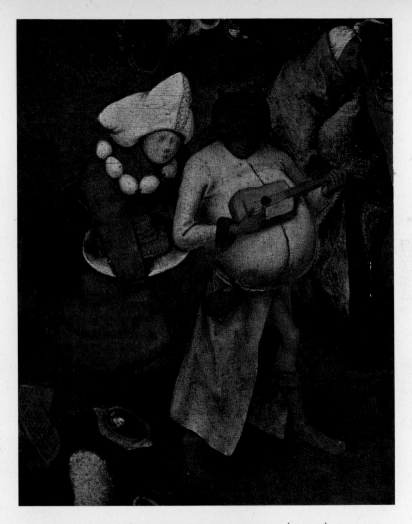

THE FIGHT BETWEEN CARNIVAL AND LENT (DETAIL), 1559.
KUNSTHISTORISCHES MUSEUM, VIENNA.

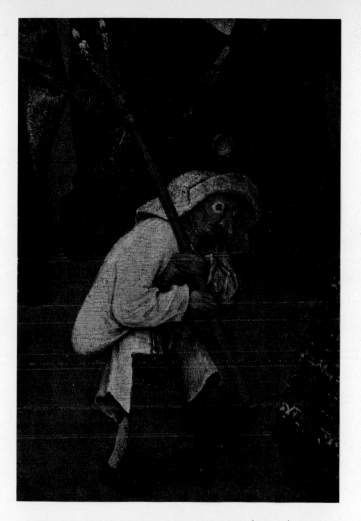

THE FIGHT BETWEEN CARNIVAL AND LENT (DETAIL), 1559.
KUNSTHISTORISCHES MUSEUM, VIENNA.

In the *Fight between Carnival and Lent* these lapses are elimi-nated. The magical power of color triumphs over a plethora of anecdotes, acting as the unifying principle between a motley throng of figures of all types and ages, hailing from very various social levels and playing their individual parts on a crowded stage. Yet this figurative multiplicity does not blind us to the dazzling sumptuosity of the painter's palette, the subtle alchemy of nuances, the glowing density of the local tones. Bright colors, gay colors, the colors of people in their "Sunday best" —and, combined and contrasted with vivid blues, acid or bluish greens, with snowy white, red supplies the major accents. A little patch of yellow sand, dappled with touches of pale green, is purposely left bare of figures; it forms an oasis of brilliant light in the middle of the picture and the starting point of two registers of color basic to the composition and spreading out across it, one consisting of greyish browns occupy-ing the lower half and the other, all in tones of ochreous grey, filling the upper zone. Together, they form a vertical backcloth against which the actors play their various parts. These actors are as clearly, forthrightly delineated as the figure studies in the *Seven Virtues* engraving; but here they no longer have that air of marionettes which gave a certain gawkiness to the figures in the *Blue Cloak*; rather, they are rendered in a wholly lifelike manner, indeed there is something almost disconcerting in the stark simplicity of their gestures, attitudes and antics.

In his illuminating description of the period that Bruegel brings so vividly to life in this picture, Lucien Febvre remarks that it was a period capable of hearing, catching the smells that hovered in the air and registering sounds, but it did not *begin by seeing*. In his intensive study of 16th-century writers one thing particularly struck our erudite historian: that "with very rare exceptions they were incapable of making a lifelike sketch of a human personality so that the reader could visualize the man in question as he was in flesh and blood." This is shrewdly said; and we find similar shortcomings in most of the painting of the time—due allowance being made for its other merits and the pleasure of the eye provided by an adroit handling of color. But Bruegel was an exception to the rule, a "triumphant harbinger of modern times." He brought to bear a virgin eye, untrammelled by convention, on the world around him. He shows us real men living out their lives. Not those who shape the destinies of nations, but men who toil and suffer and take their pleasures simply, anonymously, at the lowest social level; men without wealth or eminence. He does not pick and chose; all, such as they are, arouse his interest. Whether young or wasted by the years, healthy or infirm, frail or stalwart, well-built or mis-shapen, sad or merry, good Christians or sinners —all alike are pasture to his eyes and, for once, in *Carnival and Lent,* he brings them together in the heart of a typically Flemish village on a day of Carnival. For once only. This census-like inventory is unique of its kind, without a counterpart in the whole world of painting. It contains a wealth of contrasts —golden rule of all creative art—both simultaneous and suggestive. And behind every detail we sense a will to synthesis permeating the most meticulous analysis. This pictorial *Summa* of humanity figured forth without disguise has an instancy denied to literature.

In view of a thesis, a young French doctor has recently studied this picture from a professional angle and claimed to discover in it faithful renderings of the symptoms of a great number of diseases, physical and mental. He goes so far as to assert that only a trained physician could possibly have made such accurate diagnoses. "The fact that the great Flemish master has brought to bear on his figures the eye of an expert clinician rules out any notion of their being solely the products of his imagination"—such is Dr T. M. Torrilhon's conclusion.

53

CHILDREN'S GAMES, 1560.
KUNSTHISTORISCHES MUSEUM, VIENNA.

—

CHILDREN'S GAMES (DETAIL), 1560.
KUNSTHISTORISCHES MUSEUM, VIENNA.

CHILDREN'S GAMES (DETAIL), 1560.
KUNSTHISTORISCHES MUSEUM, VIENNA.

Though most certainly there is nothing "imaginary" in this particular work, we need not resort to any such far-fetched hypothesis in order to account for Bruegel's "realism." The truth lies elsewhere—in the rich endowment of the mind of a great creative artist who, better and more discerningly than others, could single out and body forth what was unique, peculiar to itself, in the object of his contemplation.

The leading theme came from a folk-tale that had already been pictorialized by Bosch. But quite possibly there was also an allusion to the religious conflicts of the period. According to C. G. Stridbeck the man with an enormous paunch astride a barrel who impersonates King Carnival and heads a shambling rout of masked figures, represents the Lutheran movement; while Lent, a gaunt old harridan sitting on a go-cart drawn by a monk and a nun, symbolizes the Catholic Church.

However this may be in *Carnival and Lent*, there is no trace of any such symbolism in *Children's Games*, a perfectly straight-forward work, indeed the only one of Bruegel's works to carry no recondite allusions or moral innuendos. All goes to show that it formed part of a cycle of the seasons, half of which is lost, and represented "High Summer," while *Carnival and Lent* stood for early Spring. Any other interpretation (*vide* Tietze-Conrat, Stridbeck) must certainly be ruled out.

It is clear that Bruegel had a lively sense of visual actuality, and far less of that obsession with peasant life of which he used to be accused. In *Children's Games* he shows another facet of everyday, small-town life, studied in its inception, so to say: the childhood of the rising generation. This delightful work was wholly original; attempts to link it up with any local art tradition or to trace its sources to Metsys, Bellegambe or Gossart lead nowhere. What we have here is a unique "encyclo-pedia of games," indispensable to any would-be historian of the recreations of childhood through the ages.

Alone, in couples, in threesomes or in groups, over two hundred children are disporting themselves in the marketplace of a country town, near the bank of a small stream beyond which lies open country. The landscape is superbly rendered, a green expanse in which air freely circulates, shimmering with the heat of a summer afternoon. With unfailing verve Bruegel depicts in detail a host of games, many of which we recognize, with something of a shock, as those of our own childhood: blind man's buff, leapfrog, bowls, ring-o'-roses, somersaults, trundling hoops, peg-top spinning, walking on stilts and so forth. This enumeration might easily have become monotonous, not to say tedious, if it were no more than a series of vignettes and each small scene were treated in isolation. But once again the artist has effortlessly avoided any such effect of fragmentation. To begin with, the colors are *constructive*. Less sumptuous and less modulated than in the previous picture, they are lighter, soberer, built up into a more effective compositional pattern. Against the yellowish tones of the sandy soil, blues and greens tell out and dominate the red bell-like patches of the children's garments. The contour lines of forms are more synthetic and circumscribe denser, stronger, more positive local tones. But the organic unity of the initial conception makes its presence felt in every tiny figure. None is individualized, each is a "condensation" of the crowd. When the small heads are turned towards us (usually they are shown in back view or in profile), all these little faces, round as billiard balls with two black holes for eyes, diminutive mouths and flattened noses, are curiously impersonal. It is their gestures and movements that tell us what they are after and the sort of youngsters they are: awkward or nimble, bright or backward. And they foreshadow the time when movement *in itself* was to become an object of expression.

Two later pictures carry this process a stage further: the *Land of Cockaigne* (Munich), painted in 1567, and the *Birdnester*,

Br. 18

THE LAND OF COCKAIGNE, 1567. ALTE PINAKOTHEK, MUNICH.

painted in the following year (Vienna). A comparison of these two pictures is rewarding since they show how at every stage of his brief career Bruegel made a point of following his first, instinctive impulses. For they reveal in the most convincing manner the two poles between which he always oscillated, almost as if he were seeking to demonstrate to others and to himself his ability to figure forth with equal success the new world in terms of the ancient conception of space, and vice versa. Thus in the *Land of Cockaigne* he limits space to the two dimensions

of the vertical plane upon which are presented in strong relief and in marked foreshortening three massive figures so placed as to seem to be projected bodily towards the spectator. In the *Birdnester*, on the contrary, we have a landscape prospect set out in deep recession and our gaze is led towards a distant, delicately indicated horizon. In the one case we have, if in a

THE BIRDNESTER, 1568. KUNSTHISTORISCHES MUSEUM, VIENNA.

"modernized" form, the medieval conception of space basic to *The Blue Cloak*, *Carnival and Lent* and *Children's Games*; in the other, Bruegel resorts to the technique employed in his first panoramic landscapes. In both pictures alike he seems to be testing out in terms of the visible the modifications that contemporary thought had brought to the relations between man and the world around him. And both reveal a similar economy of means oriented towards the mastery of a style, while the imagery, still that of a "topsy-turvy world," but here attuned to a gentler mood, testifies to the feelings that lay deepest, ineradicably, in the artist's heart.

The theme of the *Land of Cockaigne* derives from a Flemish proverb: "Nothing is stupider than a lazy glutton." Three men have fled from the Spanish Terror so as to bask the hours away in a land of fabulous delights. Besides their costumes, various attributes (a lance, a flail, a book) indicate their respective callings: one is a knight, the second a peasant, the third a scholar. Plunged in a sort of stupor, they seem welded to the soil, incorporated into the amply swelling curves of Mother Earth, and their bodies are boldly reduced to the elementary geometrical forms—sphere, cone and cylinder—which, after being used by Fouquet and Giotto as bases of their plastic realizations, were to become almost an obsession with Cézanne. Their limbs are tubular, their arms cylindrical, their heads and bellies round, and their thighs conical; rarely has modeling so sober produced so powerful an effect of density and monumentality. The three figures are spaced out around the foot of a docked tree-trunk on which rests a circular table, their bodies jutting out like the spokes of a wheel—a wheel that has ceased rotating. Here it would seem that the painter has combined with the above-quoted proverb the ancient notion of the "Wheel of Fortune." We owe this ingenious hypothesis to Louis Lebeer, the erudite conservator of the Cabinet des Estampes at Brussels, who has also published a hitherto unnoticed print by Pieter Balten (a contemporary of Bruegel), accompanied by an illuminating commentary and, better still, by a Netherlandish text of 1546, in which the "Luilekkerland" (Land of Cockaigne) is viewed from an angle hitherto neglected by its many commentators. "Until now this land was not known to any man save the ne'er-do-wells who first discovered it. All those who wish to go there must be men of exceeding courage and ready to undergo great hardships, for that land is cut off from the world by a very long and lofty mount of cornmeal cake through which they have to eat their way before coming to the aforesaid, most famous country, well known to scapegraces and men who have cast away every scrap of decency and virtue. For there is no greater disgrace in that country than to behave virtuously, sagely and honorably, to practise good manners and to earn one's daily bread by the labor of one's hands. The man who leads a righteous, honest life is loathed by all, and sooner or later banished from that land. Likewise he who is wise and has a good understanding is greatly scorned and none makes him welcome."

The Birdnester, too, illustrates a Flemish proverb: "The man who knows where the nest is has the knowledge, but he who takes it has the nest." In this delightful picture (there is a preliminary drawing for it in the Uffizi, Florence) Bruegel anticipates both Courbet and Corot. By a judicious handling of local tones and values, he brings out to the most telling effect the contrast between the monumentalism, clear-cut form and textural density of the central figure, which supplies the vertical axis of the composition, and the fragile beauty of the far-flung, faintly misted landscape, all in nuances and values. Were it not that these terms have been garbled and overworked in modern criticism, we would be inclined to say that in this poem in form and color we have the fulfillment of the painter's twofold vocation—impressionist and expressionist.

Here (and this is exceptional in Bruegel's work), the burly peasant is presented full-face, staring straight towards us with a vacant, impersonal gaze that seems to have no thought behind it. He has the same round eyes, flattened nose and sketchily indicated mouth that we found in the stylized youngsters of *Children's Games*. Obviously Bruegel lacks the knack of rendering a smile or the psychological content of a gaze—perhaps because he systematically refused to devote to portraiture, viewed as an independent branch of art, the same attention as was given it by contemporary humanism and by its best exponents, Moro, Key, Floris and Vermeyen. So we need not be surprised that this essentially "manly" painter, who took so little stock of the fashions of the day, never painted a female nude. Torrilhon finds in this an argument in favor of his theory that Bruegel must have been a physician; as such, the nude had no appeal for him! Be that as it may, there is no question that Bruegel

PEASANT DANCE, C. 1568. KUNSTHISTORISCHES MUSEUM, VIENNA.

PEASANT DANCE (DETAIL), C. 1568.
KUNSTHISTORISCHES MUSEUM, VIENNA.

was far from being the peasant artist, a drab incarnation of the spirit of his race (an uncouth spirit needless to say) and of his milieu (thick-witted to all accounts) that at the beginning of this century some writers and art historians who should have known better thought fit to see in him. When he broke the long silence of the Gothic epoch and ushered in the art of modern times with depictions of the boisterous rejoicings of the populace, and when he broke with a long tradition of religious art, it was because "he descended from the world of the eternal into the present"—because, in a word, he could *live himself into* all that caught his eye. And for this very reason his œuvre expresses all the more dynamically the spirit of the Northern Renaissance. He was not a painter of peasants but a great humanist—if a humanist in clogs. And this is why he could be so supreme an interpreter of everyday life and succeeded in creating a style so well adapted to the merry-makings of the populace, while there still lingered elegantly on, *diminuendo*, echoes of the genteel *fêtes* of the Burgundian patriciate.

The *Wedding Banquet* and the *Peasant Dance* (Vienna, both dating to c. 1568) form a pair; they are of the same dimensions and were almost certainly painted to the same order. This is of interest as showing it was generally recognized that Bruegel's sensibility was particularly suited to the creation of bravura pieces of this type and he had proved himself a master in this field. For the sculpturesque quality of his figures, equaling the masterly plasticity of Giotto's figurative art, does not in any way detract from the expressiveness of their attitudes, always far more natural than those of his contemporaries at Antwerp, Pieter Aertsen and Joachim Beuckelaer. And the monumentality of his forms, his supple modeling, the just balance of the masses, the vigor of his color rhythms transpose what else might be mere incidents of daily life to the level of a universal art, transcending the particular and ephemeral.

THE PROCESSION TO CALVARY (DETAIL), 1564.
KUNSTHISTORISCHES MUSEUM, VIENNA.

THE ANATOMY OF DISORDER
TESTIMONIES TO THE TIMES

I always perceive more and otherwise than I see.

JEAN-PAUL SARTRE.

CLOSELY involved as he was in the everyday life of his fellow countrymen, Bruegel could not remain indifferent to the events which were soon to steep the Netherlands in blood. As early as 1533 the behavior of the Spanish troops sent by the Emperor Charles V "to take part in the war with France" had led to a nation-wide movement of revolt, and this gained strength when Philip II outraged public opinion by increasing the powers of the inquisitors in their campaign against the Calvinist heresy (1556).

Bruegel took sides; the painter of scenes of popular life became a champion of the Resistance. In the *Monkeys* (Berlin, signed and dated 1562) we find a hardly veiled allusion to the plight of the Flemish provinces; chained in a dark arch, the two animals have their backs turned to the enchanting panoramic view of Antwerp lightly veiled in mist. Under cover of a biblical theme that superb picture, the *Battle of the Israelites and Philistines* (Vienna, signed and dated 1562) evokes the hated presence of the foreign soldiery. The setting is grandiose, a subtly conceived and finely executed reconstitution of the artist's reminiscences of the South. Painted on the eve of his marriage, it raises the possibility of Bruegel's collaboration with his future mother-in-law, the miniature painter Mayken Verhulst, believed to be the author of the famous *Banquet of the Poor* (Brunswick). Signed and dated 1562, the *Fall of the Rebel Angels* (Brussels) derives its morphology from Bosch's world of fantastic beings, its aim being to denounce human folly, incarnated in the hideous hosts of Hell launching grotesquely futile attacks on the bright, invincible archangel.

Meanwhile the situation in Flanders was deteriorating, the opposition gaining in strength and growing bolder. Huguenot emissaries now were preaching in broad daylight and in *St John the Baptist Preaching* (Budapest, signed and dated 1566) we have a discreet tribute to their courage. The country was flooded with pamphlets printed at the headquarters of the underground Calvinist movement; there were tavern brawls between Flemish patriots and Spanish soldiers; hundreds of suspects were rounded up, tortured, burnt at the stake. Once again Bruegel had recourse to Boschian "dialectic" in his *Dulle Griet* (1564, Mayer van den Bergh Museum, Antwerp), whose indictment of Spanish brutality is disguised by the archaism of the subject and its reference to a popular saying, "When you go to Hell, go sword in hand." This is connected with the legend of St Margaret vanquishing the devil, and immediately beside the gigantic form of Dulle Griet ("Mad Meg") forcing her way through the myrmidons of hell, we see the "best of Margarets known to the world, binding the devil to a mattress." The work is purposely ambivalent and lends itself to several interpretations. But all the allusions latent in it seem to center on a basic theme; bewildering as is the overall effect, the action advances by clean-cut successive episodes in the manner of the medieval mystery play. And what gives its paradoxical coherence to this seemingly chaotic picture, its unifying principle, is the element of fire. Through a throng of monstrous creatures, spawn of the atavistic fears that haunt the mental underworld, Dulle Griet strides boldly forward, carrying the long sword of the giants of mythology, wearing a helmet and breastplate, her eyes flashing fire, while from her gaping lips issues the song of the eternal tyrant, *wil je niet je moet wel* ("whether you like it or not, you *shall*"). She carries baskets crammed with loot and seems completely indifferent to the havoc she has spread around her, lit up on all sides by the glare of distant conflagrations. Clearly

THE FALL OF THE REBEL ANGELS, 1562.
MUSÉES ROYAUX DES BEAUX-ARTS, BRUSSELS.

this apocalyptic figure, central point of the composition, has a symbolic meaning; as Minnaert points out, she incarnates the spirit of oppression and brutality—elemental malevolence without a spark of pity. Two forlorn monkeys penned behind iron bars reinforce the artist's message. The horrors of the Occupation are firstfruits of the "Disasters of War," and *Dulle Griet*, anticipating *Guernica*, has a like dramatic intensity.

Br. 25

DULLE GRIET, 1564.
MAYER VAN DEN BERGH MUSEUM, ANTWERP.

DULLE GRIET (DETAIL), 1564. MAYER VAN DEN BERGH MUSEUM, ANTWERP.

Its subterranean source is a meditation on the significance of
fire. "Fire," as Bachelard has observed, "suggests the desire
of change, of speeding up the march of time, of bringing
all life to its conclusion—or its aftermath. Thus these musings
on fire acquire an arresting and dramatic significance, since they
give human destiny a wider purport, link up the little with the

men rounded up by Spanish mounted troops, Nature plays her part in the human tragedy. Clad in her springtime finery at the starting-point of the procession, she gradually loses all her beauty as the crowd moves on towards the bleak desolation of the fatal hilltop. Though it had Flemish and Italian precedents, this picture (of which Van Mander merely said that "it looks very natural") differs from them *toto caelo*, not only as regards its iconography but also, and above all, by the scope and sensitivity of the artist's visualization of the scene. The eye is led across a maze of colorful incidents locked within the far-flung triangle of a strictly unitary viewpoint—both an optical and a figurative unity. Here Bruegel seems to be putting into practice his accumulated knowledge of man and nature, of concepts and of figures; all his ruling interests—intellectual, social, plastic and painterly—converge, guided by the master's hand, upon this crowded scene. For the composition merits careful study. How effectively, for instance, yet how discreetly, does the local color set off the bright red of the soldiers' tunics! And how remarkable is Bruegel's handling of the soil, which here serves as a backdrop, spangled with myriads of small starry patches of green, brown and pink, no longer executed with the minute precision, the smooth enamel finish and glossy greens favored by the Primitives! Here we have the beginnings of an art of "becoming," of incessant mobility, answering to the agitation of the tiny figures fanning out in all directions and filling the entire picture with sparkling, vibrant life. Upon a stormy sky a bird is wheeling, a bird of ill omen, one of those carrion crows that haunt places of execution. But it has also a plastic function and as a focal point, high in air, suggests the vastness of space—creating the same effect of fathomless depth as does the bird flying over the frozen ponds in *Hunters in the Snow*. And this sense of the awe-inspiring immensity of space is borne out also by the rendering of the sky itself.

THE PROCESSION TO CALVARY, 1564.
KUNSTHISTORISCHES MUSEUM, VIENNA.

THE PROCESSION TO CALVARY, DETAIL: THE MAGDALEN, 1564.
KUNSTHISTORISCHES MUSEUM, VIENNA.

THE CONVERSION OF ST PAUL, DETAIL: HORSEMAN, 1567.
KUNSTHISTORISCHES MUSEUM, VIENNA.

The clouds are handled with a remarkable feeling for expressive values and at the same time conform to a carefully thought-out design; lowering, leaden-hued storm clouds hollow out space and thrust back to an infinite distance the white and dark blue cloud-rack billowing around them. M. Damisch has recently given us a magisterial survey of the part played by clouds as "plastic tools"—a work that no one interested in the means of pictorial construction can afford to disregard. That the author has overlooked Bruegel's remarkable contribution in this domain is regrettable but perhaps understandable. There is no question that, while in this great picture (as elsewhere) the cloud "introduces a new dimension into the composition," it also helps the painter to free himself from any stereotyped, theatrical presentation of the scene. Much more might be said about the *Procession to Calvary*, but we shall confine ourselves to drawing the reader's attention to the group of mourners in the foreground (St John upholding the weeping Virgin, attended by the Holy Women). This group, punctuated with passages of vivid yellow, illustrates the persistence of Gothic formalism, tending towards mannerism, and in both theme and style, seems somewhat out of keeping with the intense dramatic actuality of the picture as a whole.

Meanwhile the insurrectionary movement was making alarming headway in all parts of the country, as a result both of the prevailing political anarchy and of catastrophic economic conditions; industry had come to a standstill and there was widespread unemployment. A furious outburst of iconoclasm in 1566 was accompanied by a tidal wave of destruction; bands of fanatical marauders roamed the countryside burning down churches, looting monasteries, slashing pictures, mutilating statues. Philip II took prompt action and on October 30, 1566, the Spanish regiments stationed in Lombardy set out for the insurgent provinces. They had to cross the Alps—an arduous

THE CONVERSION OF ST PAUL, 1567. KUNSTHISTORISCHES MUSEUM, VIENNA.

and exhausting performance now that winter was coming on. Bruegel employed a Gospel theme as the pretext for his grandiose evocation of an army on the march through a wild, mountainous country. The *Conversion of St Paul* (signed and dated 1567) is his most elaborate, most fully plotted-out composition. It is given pride of place in that room in the Kunsthistorisches Museum, Vienna, which has the unique distinction of containing no less than fourteen pictures by the great Flemish master, all restored to their pristine brightness by judicious cleaning. Van Mander speaks of this work, and what struck him most were "the very beautiful rocks" that figure in it. But surely there was far more to admire: the softly dappled foliage of the fir-trees, the telling counterpoint of masses, and the disposition of the long straggling line of human figures, cavalry and foot soldiers, marshaled with fine precision in a space that taxed the artist's ingenuity to the utmost. Indeed it would seem that everything in the composition is governed by a single overriding concern: that of unifying the theme by trapping every detail in the serried meshes of a wide perspective vista. In no other work by Bruegel do we find so many indications of spatial recession: the vast plain and the city, dwarfed by distance, seen on the left between a wide rift in the cliffs; the troops streaming up from a ravine and steadily growing larger as they approach us; the criss-cross patterning of the lances; the men on horseback shown in close-up in the foreground on the right; then diminishing once again as they move away into the depths of the mountain range. And everywhere the color, subdued or brilliant, follows the changes imposed by geometrical perspective on the forms. Here, as so often in his large-scale works, Bruegel has given no prominence to the scene which is the nominal subject. This is the conversion of Saul, the Hellenized Jew, on his way from Jerusalem to Damascus, when suddenly "there shined about him a light from heaven" and, stricken with fear, he fell off his horse and heard a voice saying, "Saul, Saul, why persecutest thou me?" Like the scene of Christ staggering under the burden of the Cross in the *Procession to Calvary*, this episode occupies the exact center of the picture. Yet it is only an incident of the day's journey, and the soldiers march steadily ahead as if nothing had happened.

The *Massacre of the Innocents* (c. 1567, Vienna) shows the Duke of Alva's troops at their bloodthirsty task and it contains,

Van Mander tells us, "much that actually happened, for example a peasant family begging one of the murderous soldiers to spare the life of a child he is about to kill, the mothers fainting in their grief, and other scenes done straight from life." The setting is a snowbound Brabantine village and the frozen stillness of nature makes a telling foil to the brutal violence of the foreign soldiers, who are mounted on fiery thoroughbreds depicted with a mastery worthy of Pisanello. All the same, the essentially decorative quality of the handling raises some problems as regards this work. When we compare it with the nearby pictures we cannot fail to notice that the execution is less fluent, there is even a certain stiffness in the drawing, movement is arrested in the gestures, and the style seems relatively conventional. In short, as Henri Hymans has pointed out, it lacks the finesse we expect of Bruegel. Charles de Tolnay shares the doubts expressed by Max J. Friedländer and Edouard Michel as to the authenticity of the *Massacre*. Grossmann believes it to have been painted in Bruegel's workshop and partially retouched by him, asserting that the pentimenti disclosed in X-ray photographs are proof of this. We, however, after a thorough inspection of the picture in full light, are convinced that this picture is not the work of a copyist or studio assistant. The linework may seem stiff but there is nothing hesitant about it, and only Bruegel could have supplied the brilliant color orchestration. We find saturated tones, vermilions, yellows, greens and white, and color harmonies that assuredly derive from the palette of the master of *Children's Games* and which here serve as the staffage of a brilliantly original composition, the work of a creator in full possession of his means. That there is, perhaps, a certain lack of forcefulness is due to one of those temporary lowerings of "working pressure" which so often befall creative artists—unless it means that we have here a second version of a work that has not yet been traced. As a

THE MASSACRE OF THE INNOCENTS, C. 1567.
KUNSTHISTORISCHES MUSEUM, VIENNA.

matter of fact, Van Puyvelde believes he has discovered it in
Baron Descamps' collection at Brussels, while Grossmann
makes out a case for the *Massacre* in Hampton Court. The dimensions of the Vienna picture signed BRUEG. (116 by 160 cm.)
are much the same as those of the Brussels version (115 by
164.5 cm.) on which is painted the signature BRUEGEL 15..;
the Hampton Court version, which seems to have been cut down

on top and on the left (109.2 by 154.9 cm.), bears no signature. But—and this has its importance—the two last-named pictures have more in common, iconographically, and also show much the same divergencies from the Vienna version (e.g. the placing of the horses in the lefthand bottom corner, and the birds flying overhead), except for one detail which, in the Hampton Court picture, completely changes the significance of one of the most dramatic scenes. The child whom a soldier has

THE NUMBERING AT BETHLEHEM, 1566.
MUSÉES ROYAUX DES BEAUX-ARTS, BRUSSELS.

just seized by the arm, to the despair of the father and mother kneeling before the officers on horseback (as noted by Van Mander in the Vienna or the Brussels picture), has been here replaced by a young calf! Since there can be no question of an over-painting (Grossmann would certainly have detected it in his X-ray examination) this odd "correction" must have been the work of a copyist. In any case it would be an excellent idea to place the three works side by side so as to have an opportunity of studying and comparing them objectively without any *parti pris* or nationalistic bias—unless of course we subscribe to M. Blanchot's view that "all masterpieces tend to be no more than brilliant traces of the passage of an anonymous, impersonal creative power, that of Art in its entirety."

There can be no question that it was not mere caprice that led Bruegel to take for the theme of one of his major works the *Numbering at Bethlehem* (Brussels). Here he selected from the repertory of the mystery plays a subject that lent itself to illustrating, in an indirect manner, one of the darkest hours in the history of his country. The picture is dated 1566, the year in which the iconoclasts destroyed so many public buildings and works of art. The ruins of a castle in the background— Grossmann has identified this detail with a drawing Bruegel made in 1562 at the gates of Amsterdam—symbolize the havoc wrought by them. "All went to be taxed," we read in the Gospel of St Luke, "everyone into his own city. And Joseph also went up from Galilee unto the city of David, which is called Bethlehem, to be taxed with Mary his espoused wife." We see Joseph and Mary arriving at Bethlehem—but this Bethlehem is a Flemish village on the banks of a frozen river. And the holy figures, given the "local color," pass unnoticed in the crowd. Children are skating, sliding, tumbling on the ice, while outside the local inn, "The Green Crown," a group of villagers is waiting in stolid resignation to hear that the war-tax

CONTENTS

THIS VOLUME, THE TWENTY-NINTH OF THE COLLECTION "THE
TASTE OF OUR TIME", WAS PRODUCED BY THE TECHNICAL STAFF
OF EDITIONS D'ART ALBERT SKIRA, FINISHED THE FIFTEENTH
DAY OF SEPTEMBER NINETEEN HUNDRED AND FIFTY-NINE.

TEXT AND ILLUSTRATIONS BY

SKIRA

COLOR STUDIOS
AT IMPRIMERIES RÉUNIES S.A., LAUSANNE.

PLATES ENGRAVED BY GUEZELLE AND RENOUARD, PARIS.

PHOTOGRAPHS BY

*Hans Hinz, Basel (pages 26, 34, 35, 50, 51, 56, 57, 66, 68, 80, 81, 83, 86, 91, 96,
103, 107, 110, 111, 112, 119, 123 and title-page), Henry B. Beville, Washington
(pages 30, 31, 108, 109), Claudio Emmer, Milan (pages 116, 122), Louis Laniepce,
Paris (page 75), Walter Steinkopf, Berlin (page 40), Karel Neubert, Prague
(page 101), and by the photographic services of the Prado, Madrid (pages 92, 93)
and of the Staatsgemäldesammlung, Berlin-Dahlem (page 45).*

PRINTED IN SWITZERLAND

LIST OF COLORPLATES